The Broken Clock:
An Examination of People and Society

By
Leonard Swafford-Donald
Foreword by Tony Smith

DEDICATION

This work is sincerely dedicated to the memories, sacrifices, and strengths of Ida B. Wells-Barnett and Wilma Rudolph. Everyone should take the time to learn the stories of these two lives, for they are stories of unbelievable willpower, love, and determination.

This work is also dedicated to any and all who show mercy, exercise forgiveness, and take the time to learn how to deal justly. Those who energize their ideas into meaningful, tangible things that assist in the growth of the human principle. If this cloak fits about your shoulders, then push and shove your ideas until they explode into a great, new, world.

-The Author

The Broken Clock: An Examination of People and Society
© 2015 Master Builder Publications

ISBN-13: 978-1-50231-9944
ISBN-10: 1-50231-9942

Published by Master Builder Publications
10 East Brookline Street #43, Boston, MA 02118 USA

Printed in the United States of America

Contents

Contributors

Alex Jeanty
Lawanda Swafford
J. Jabir Pope
Deborah Raye
Zachariah Bush
The New Start Project
Master Builders Empowerment Group
Tanji Donald
Naeem Miles
Tony Smith
Stephen P. Engley
Alisha Donald
Bill Himelhoch
Mary Ellen Flannery
Cherish CowanRaye
Alex Garcia
Jeffrey Anthony
.William "Kasim" Lane

FOREWORD
By Tony Smith

Lost Time of the Broken Clock

Imagine if we had no way of telling time. How chaotic would the world be? Being that our world is so fast pace and automatic, most of our lives are organized around a daily schedule. We rely on our schools, public transportation systems, and hospitals, which are organized around schedules. A clock is a measurement device of time. If the clock is broken, then congruency becomes unharmonious. Time is the continued existence of past, present, and future. We cannot recover time loss, but we can embrace the time present, and plan for the time that will give us the opportunity to exhale all of our divine, giving potential.

Potential is the discovery and release of our talents and skills, that we were giving when we were released to the earth. Potential is not based on what is, but what can be. Every effective leader is a product of released potential.

Reentry resident and prolific author, Leonard Swafford Donald's latest book, "The Broken Clock" explores the high cost of incarceration and its direct relation to poverty, scarce leadership, violence, and disorder in our community. In Leonard's first book, "Master Builder: A Guide To Enrich Your Life", he helped the reader to reflect on their own personal development, which he revealed was a critical necessity to overall systematic change for marginalized and oppressed people. In this book, Leonard is exploring how big and small players in the system use time as punishment; punishment that leads to the perpetuation of the marginalization of our communities, families, and individuals.

I have had the privilege and honor to work beside Leonard over the past year. I have witnessed first-hand his ability to redeem time lost by the broken clock. He has successfully journeyed through: returning home from prison, persevering through life setbacks, dealing with the loss of loved ones, stubbornly being committed to completing his education, and getting involved in his community through direct participation in organizations like New Start Project. He is the epitome of cultivated potential that develops capable leadership. Effective leadership is essential in repairing our community's broken clock. In this book, his vision for how we repair our Broken Clock can produce harmony, order, prosperity, and peace in our community.

We must influence the clock's big hand to be in harmony with the small hand, so that we can accurately measure the times in which we are trying to make sense of, understanding who we are, and where we are going in this world. If there is anyone who can share with us what it is like to live in a time of brokenness, and yet provide us a blueprint to a path of wholeness, it is Leonard Swafford Donald!

I am the Executive Director of New Start Project, which is a reentry advocacy organization. Through my work, I can confirm that the broken clock produces fear. The broken clock produces the fear of rejection, the fear of failure, and the fear of success. The big hand of the system has led to unnecessary incarcerations. Incarcerations have led to a broken life cycle and a revolving door of incarceration. The broken life cycle of obtaining education, creating a family, and obtaining a livable wage career. This has caused the small hand on the clock to suddenly stop at the darkest hour of the night.

This book summons us to arise just before the dawn and seize the moment of time that has provided us with the opportunity to understand ourselves and the systematic barriers that hinder us from being all that we can be. We can begin to repair and wind up the clock and restore harmony and congruency to our environment that leads to prosperity and order. Not just financial prosperity, but the flourishing of the human soul and spirit. Not just the order of physical safety, but the order of man's dominion over his environment, instead of being subjected to it.

In conclusion, "The Broken Clock" compels me to share my favorite quote by Robert F. Kennedy, a man who dedicated his public life to repairing the broken clock of the systematic oppression of racial injustice, poverty, and classism. He said, "Some people see things as they are and ask why? But I dream things that have never been and ask why not? The dream will not be easy to birth to reality. The repairs will be costly and require a great sacrifice. But our unshakeable resolve is our faithful heart and our deepest satisfaction is in our suffering. For Martin Luther King Jr. once said, "Undeserved suffering was redemptive."

With the help of this book, I can boldly contend that no matter the burden, we will bear the burden again and again in the noble endeavor of setting the oppressed free. Free from injustice, free from poverty, free from violence, free from incarceration, free from stigma, free from being hoodwinked, and free from the broken clock.

<u>INTRODUCTION</u>

There are some who believe that the burden of explaining things rests on their shoulders, and in so doing, this notion projects a cloak of disbelief over those who have yet to establish their "shoulders".

It is not my assignment to explain anything. Nor is it my point to be accusatory. Sadly, the burden bearers, those whose words and works heretofore have been received with praise and utilized as a standard against which all other arguments are measured, have built their points on unfounded incidences and well woven, regurgitated facts.

Facts, once they become interspersed with opinion, or worse, backed by an agenda that purposely disregards other facts that assist in stabilizing an argument, are no longer facts. They become the machinations of someone attempting to "make things clear" from their perspective, and this does not always translate into that which is true. A pinch of falsehood contaminates an ocean of truth, only because the truth has no retort, no force to stand against it, while false notions and lies can be broken, overwhelmed, and respectfully destroyed.

A host of social voices have a tendency to speak from the top down when addressing issues that affect segments of our population that they have never been a member of. This, to me, appears disingenuous, and on some levels unfair. A fair assessment of anything ill, especially one of a social import, should have its origins amongst the people it affects the most.

The difficulty with speaking from the bottom up is that it places one in a precarious position, a position that always has to be defended. For example, a person addicted to drugs can tell us the harmful effects of addiction, the losses associated with it, and the burden it places on their family, community, and themselves. However, in so doing, they expose themselves and the source of their misfortune to scrutiny and perhaps ridicule. How many of us are willing to do this? How many of us are willing to admit that we are weak? How many of us are endearing enough to swap our discretion to reveal the truth?

In contrast, the scientist, the one who studies the physiological and socio-economical aftermath of drug abuse, can write volumes and give lectures in spades in regards to his or her "profession". All of this can be done in the name of research and will not place the aforementioned person in an adverse index, even if they sway far from the truth. Their "professionalism" shields them.

When I assert a title referencing an examination of people and society, it is because I am a person, and I am now in the process of understanding the concept of what society truly is. This is not a work reliant on what I want people to believe, rather it is a work reliant on people making an effort to focus a clear lens on society as a whole.

I do not boast an extensive academic resume, nor have I ever assumed the role of author par excellence. This work is, by design, an attempt to respectfully expose the systems that function in society, and the people that they have the most severe impact on. With this in mind, I will not browbeat you, Dear Reader, with statistics or the high-handed speech of some immortal pedagogue.

For this walk I enlisted the assistance of those "who raise dust with their feet"; those who strive from the bottom up while maintaining a dignity that can only come from making mistakes and moving forward from the errors of life, even if those errors have placed them in an unfavorable circumstance.

CHAPTER 1
TRUE CRIMES

*"The court is focused on giving law
enforcement every possible tool and every
degree of power necessary to seek out,
apprehend, and find criminals."*
-David Harris, *Law Professor,
University of Toledo*

To Give All and Have Nothing

It will suffice here to point out that
millions of people in America have had some
kind of encounter with law enforcement.
Some favorable, while others veer to the
extreme contrast. Bearing in mind that law
enforcement is a pugnacious extension of the
criminal justice system, one cannot evade the
ominous reality that laws are endorsed so
that arrests can be made, convictions can be
upheld, and people are sent to prison. These
are facts that we know, statistical and
otherwise.

There are segments of society that the criminal justice system works for, and clearly, there are segments of society that the criminal justice system works against. If a neighborhood street gang engages in what is deemed to be criminal activity, the public outcry does not invoke the DEA, or the ATF and E to stem the flow of illicit narcotics and unlawful machine guns into the community to *prevent* crime. Rather, the public outcry is for the *people* of the street gang to be removed from the community, while bullets and crack cocaine continues to flow, waiting for the next ship of fools to come along and make use of them. The aforementioned unfortunate reality begs one to question the motives and the role that law enforcement plays in actually "enforcing the law".

We the people must address the most basic problems that society faces on a daily basis. When a sixteen year old can find and procure guns, ammunition, and drugs in less than a three-block radius, is he the problem, or is he the utensil that is used to vivify the greater problem; the problem that finds its origins in malfeasance on behalf of powers greater than him; powers that make the submachine gun in his knapsack look like a raggedy, handmade slingshot.

When a person acts to the contrary of the laws of society, they become subject to the punishment of society. Every law that counteracts criminal behavior, on its face, is not inhumane. More importantly, people must feel safe in their respective communities. No person should feel as if they live under a constant threat or in the way of imminent danger. The stark reality is that crime does exist; there is a potential for violence and theft, arson and vandalism. The question is: Why does this *potential* exist?

No person can forecast the future. What we can do is rationalize how and why incidences of crime takes place, and what is the root cause before we fanatically holler out for justice. This tendency to rail for punitive measures distracts us from the larger issue, an issue that is not unmarried in its scope, however multitudinous and far-reaching.

When the public wants justice it means that they want someone to punish; someone to despise and discredit, as if this somehow eliminates the purported crime or the *reason* behind the crime. In actuality, it widens the gulf between the problem and the solution. This fact leads to yet another fundamental question: are laws enacted to deter criminal behavior or to punish people for criminal behavior?

No law can stop crime. There is no research whatsoever to indicate that punitive laws deter people from committing crime. However, there is evidence that supports the fact that the restructuring of certain social policies, such as enfranchisement, employment, and the availability of affordable housing, greatly reduces crime in communities where it is reported. Incarceration, as a result of a person being arrested, does not dull the hum of criminal behavior, nor does it eradicate crime, nor does it cast a spell to erase the social rabbit holes that leads to crime.

We cannot allow the frontier of ignorance to expand. If we know that every part of our society has external components that are readily visible to all, then we have to acknowledge the fact that there is an intricate, not so easily visible counterpart. Conspiracy theory be damned, there are elements in our society that do not favor the growth of certain groups. This breakdown in social intercourse, not surprisingly, produces desperate conditions that in turn produces alienated and angry people. Thus, the criminal justice system and its laws are viewed as some evil horde that forces people to lurch from crisis to crisis without any intervention or assistance, unless they want to be subject to society's abyss.

What we prepare for is usually what we get. When we prepare an environment where prisons are constructed more expediently than factories or community colleges, what are we actually *preparing* for? A tremendous amount of resources, energy, and planning goes into punishing people for going against the rules of society, as opposed to these things being used for a poised and integrated examination as to why people compromise their sense of right and wrong in the first place.

We give all and have nothing, and then wonder why? We enact and enforce reprehensible policies that break the will of already broken people and expect them to believe in everything except survival. This is an ideal that can only reduce people to despair.

It is true, no lie, certain, and to be depended upon, that disagreement among people leads to the malfunction of the society in which we live. When the eye through which we look at each other is obscured, we have no choice, however unfortunate, but to look forward to disorder. When parents are raising their children in an environment where they can get a place in the morgue or a prison identification number before they can get a job or a high school diploma, then we have to expect the collapse of all things considered humane, as well as the disenchantment of people who once believed in freedom, justice, and equality.

Areas of Heightened Crime

Alberto Burneko put it best when he said that "America is a serial brutalizer of black and brown people" in his article in Deadspin, *The American Criminal Justice System is Not Broken*, saying that it is doing what it is designed to do. There is a long history, slavery controlled black bodies in a strict manner, using the ideal of livestock to forget that they were trafficking in humans, as we found out ignorance is only so strong. Emancipation lived and died within a generation, progress quickly rolled back, de facto laws re-enslaving some, but did not fail to stifle most. The sixties and seventies brought these de facto laws to the forefront. Today with industrial efficiency the processing and incarceration of black bodies is done with precision and with the same moral flourishes of both slavery and Jim Crow. America's racial history is continuously filled with racial laws, and the absence of such would be a truly remarkable thing.

Let's begin by addressing the push and pull and myths about civil rights in America. In hindsight it is easy to confuse success from desegregation and the creation of a post racial society. After emancipation, the popular explosion of support subsided those who have a long-term social stake in discrimination made long-term investments in rolling back progressive advances or circumventing progressive proscriptions. After Jim Crow, it was easy to assume that progress had advanced since African Americans were now equal on paper.

Token African Americans in key positions in both the political process and criminal justice system obfuscated this process. That consensus of agreement of colorblindness in law did not clean the American soul of the violence that it harbored against black folk, though it did make most people think it had. All it meant was that transparent and unapologetic racial discrimination was now illegal.

These laws targeting racial discrimination were put into place to defend in court a person's rights, but laws do not exist in a vacuum. Today we have made people of color reside in high crime areas in spite of the hard work put forward in the civil rights movement. Some of the problem is that black culture has been targeted with increasingly punitive laws and social mores which bring them stricter scrutiny from law enforcement and increased negative contact with the criminal justice system. Much of the reason for this seems to be a case of scapegoating in order to create political capital and funding for police.

Historically, in the United States, this level of control has existed before, though in different forms. The Chinese smoked opium, as was per their cultural tradition to do so, while opium was criminalized, the European form of ingesting opium Laudanum, was still available. It was a matter of economics, the Chinese were moving into the job market of white workers in the area. Racial laws do not need to be racist in language to disproportionately affect people who are vulnerable legally.

When the Crack epidemic hit US cities, legislation was put into effect with the same results of the San Francisco opium laws. Crack laws in the United States were 100 times more severe than cocaine laws and those convicted were majority African American. Cocaine and Crack, chemically the same drug, were viewed differently. Cocaine in culture is viewed with relative respect associated with success and riches, crack is associated with blackness and violence. Mandatory minimums, high level crack cocaine laws, ravaged black neighborhoods as much as, if not more as the drug itself. It targeted people who were in desperate need of treatment, and condemned them like a vengeful God to the swelling underworld that was being created in America.

The spectrums of legality and illegality in the Drug War are very much associated with race and privilege. Marijuana went through similar growing pains as crack when the drug was first associated with Blacks and ebbed with the ushering of the haze filled dorm rooms of the sixties. When young white kids started smoking dope, federal studies were made showing that marijuana was not as evil as previously thought. Additionally, in the bathroom cabinets of suburban grandmothers with abused Ativan, opiates and sleeping medications are not ransacked and the property seized because of a drug violation. Geography and society matter a great deal when it comes to areas of heightened crime. When you define a particular people or class with "areas of heightened crime", the police are there to follow.

Areas of heightened crime are therefore allowed less civil rights than areas that are looser in standards of criminality. In these areas any sort of minor criminal infractions are addressed to the letter of the law. Police are trained to make pre-textual stops for minor traffic violations and leverage them into consent drug searches.[1] J-walking, impeding the progress of a walkway, not using a turn signal at the correct distance, makes most people outside of their homes vulnerable to minor and even

---

[1] Operation Pipeline

imagined infractions. These are based on the theory that if minor infractions are strictly enforced, then major ones will be less likely to occur.

This method of unusual search and seizure is used to search for criminal behavior like drugs or weapons, although many people need to be searched in order to find a criminal candidate. This parade of guilty people gives the false impression of a criminal problem, though it is a product of systematic police stops for particular crimes in particular neighborhoods where people are given less rights. It is arguable whether all police feel these practices are helping the communities that these "criminals" are from, though they are most certainly financially connected to arresting vulnerable populations.

More arrests mean more federal funding for War on Drug packages leading to searching in communities that have implicitly less civil rights. Because of a history of a lack of redress in criminal justice and intensified often unrestricted violence on racial minorities, these affected people rarely want to extend their contact with this system with a complaint. Making entire geographies that are higher crime areas by design to keep payroll and the lights on in police station is a way that an entire people is kept illegal. Police forces also get revenue through money in drug seizures, property gotten through drug crimes, where the property can be considered guilty of crime no matter what the conduct of the owner was. This incentive is to find drugs and claim the cars or homes of people who may not even be party to the crime. Not only is redress less likely if you are poor, but the criminal justice system has a financial stake in keeping the drug war alive.

But the statistics were never part of the decision to make a War on Drugs. One part was fear, in rolling out the Reagan version of the War on Drugs, the crack epidemic fueled the bonfire which became "tough on crime." The fire spread from the republican stump speech mainstay, to a democratic mainstay as Dukakis, the democratic nominee who was decimated for being "soft on crime." For twenty years this continued, with bills like truth in sentencing, crack laws, mandatory minimums, three strikes, life without parole, drug crimes upping the ante while politicians fell all over themselves to continue to send people to jail for political gain. The jails overflowed from 800,000 to 2.7 million people with about the same amount affected with lasting legal designations after incarceration.

Incarceration is not the end of the payment to society, making it effectively illegal to be incarcerated and extending and deepening the high crime area around a person. Once released (if you are lucky enough not to revisit), you can be barred from all sorts of federal programs, work opportunities, licenses (including drivers), and you are most likely left to defunded rehabilitation programs and inchoate citizen's advocacy programs. If your family is in government housing you are not allowed to live with them, if you do they will be evicted. You lose the right to vote depending on state laws. These realities are what is below the tip of the iceberg of incarceration. Making it in America is tough when the value of your personhood has been chipped away until all you can do is provide jobs to criminal justice and their contractors through taxpayer dime.

The final stage of a high crime area is very likely also the first stage, where the lack of rights lead a person to have a larger percentage of options to make ends meet that are based on illegal activity. Feeding the person back into the system once again.

Finally, the communities, these geographies of heightened crime are far too important if we are to call ourselves champions of human rights. These people should not be the raw material that provide power to our elite and jobs where jobs are not needed. Fight for the people who are here in our country who are being destroyed by our apathy and privilege. Shrink the size of our police force and criminal systems, end the War on Drugs and ratchet down the police forces. Today take a step forward by making it legal again to be black and make it legal to be poor. The wounds of racial violence and death can be healed.

-Stephen P. Engley, Insightful Human Being

CHAPTER 2
CRIMINAL JUSTICE

From the Inside

In this section I found it important to hear the voices of those that are currently in the grasp of the criminal justice system. This is in no way an attempt on my behalf to cloak the reality of the compromise of what is deemed right and wrong in our society. On the contrary, it is an attempt to uncover how the policies and procedures of the aforementioned system does more harm than good, and the need to rethink how the warehousing of people reflects the severe collapse of "criminal justice".

As an OG who has been doing time in the Massachusetts system for decades, I have seen the evolution in policy, character, focus, and it is not pretty. The "divide and conquer" game is in full effect.

The move from Human Services to Public Safety has created a climate of hatred, abuse, and blindness that is dangerous beyond criminal. The collaboration between politicians, media, and law enforcement has transformed America, in general, and prison, in particular, into the new Russia/South Africa.

If you were to ask any man or woman walking the street if they have ever seen the media corner the President and ask him about the state of the country and what is going on in the world, they will say, "Sure". Ask them if they have ever seen the media run up on the Governor and asked him about what's going on in the state, and they will say, "Of course". Ask them if they have ever seen the media run up on the Mayor and ask about what's going on in the cities and towns, and they will probably say, "Sure all the time". Then ask them if they have ever seen the media run up on the Commissioner of Corrections and inquire as to what is going on in the prisons, and you will get a pause accompanied by a vacant look in their eyes followed by a, "Come to think of it, no." Cynical prisoners and free people alike will say it is because people don't want to know and/or they don't care.

Optimists however, would point out that, out of view is out of mind but, people do want to know. Some because they care, some because they are simply nosy, but people do want to know. So don't believe the hype. It is the propaganda of those who most benefit from the secrets that are kept about prison life and its real effects on poor people, people of color, and the segment of society whose only crime is, they love us. The bean counter mentality that declare it is cheaper to let us die rather than provide quality or even decent medical care, is the same mentality that allows spending conservatively seven cents per prisoner per meal, but bills the taxpayer for steak and caviar. Hollowed out programs that are purported to aid in reentry with large federal grants attached to them are but a few of the secrets that Mary and Joe Citizen are unaware of.

Equally important is that society is, and has been, in the dark about where a lot of their rights come from. For example, citizens have a right to privacy because prisoners fought for that. They have a right to remain silent if arrested; access to an attorney free of charge if they cannot afford one; to be secure in their home, property, and person from unfair intrusion by law enforcement, and the list goes on.

I am in prison doing forever for a crime that God, and an honest examination of the record will reveal I did not do. In the United States of America, how can that be? Furthermore, how can it be that the highest court in the land would respond to such an injustice by simply saying, "We refuse to hear it". It is almost as if they are children with their fingers stuck in their ears.

The internal hypocrisy is all about dollars and job security. Break up the families of poor people, target them for crime and convictions, all the while creating job security for correctional officials, their family and offspring. Now contrast that with this: if I had a seventeen-year old son, he would not be allowed to visit me on his own, as he would be considered a minor. But, arrest him at that same age and he is magically transformed into an adult, and can now be placed in the cell right next to me.

"Officials" get to raise their children within the system with all the government benefits, the only interference being the shield from any blemishes on their records. I get to raise my children in prison visiting rooms with *them* interfering when my child wants a piggy-back ride. I live in an environment where the loss of a loved one is often met with insensitivity, callousness, and hardheartedness. Men who have built bonds that span decades, crying on each other's shoulders during times of grief, celebrating the achievements of their children and loved ones through grade school, junior high and so on, are not even allowed to write a letter to each other if they are transferred to a different facility within the same Department of Corrections.

Finally, the crown jewel of the criminal justice system is hypocrisy. Powerless people tend to use the phrase, "just us", but the more accurate term is "just them". They believe just because they say it, it is so. This hypocrisy comes in damaging forms and is widespread. In fact, it is policy. The idea, for example, is if five, fully-geared correctional officers advance on me and I defend myself, I can, and will be charged with assault. However, if they get their hands around my neck and choke me to oblivion, they are restraining me, and the courts will excuse their every move.

Those that are *them*, on those very rare occasions when the cuffs are placed on their wrists; the cops, politicians, judges, etc.; They are the ones that scream the loudest, "I have rights, you can't do this to me! I resent being treated like a common criminal! Don't you know who I am!?!" The undertone of course being, *I am in the club. This treatment is for other people, not us, because we are the "them".*

It is only when <u>WE</u> remember that this is a government *OF THE PEOPLE, BY THE PEOPLE*, and *FOR THE PEOPLE* and to act accordingly that this madness stops. It is our move **REAL PEOPLE**. Lord knows it has been long enough for *THEM*.

-J. Jabir Pope, Thinker, Author, Seeker of Justice

I started stealing cars and dirt bikes around the age of thirteen with my friends in Boston. At the time, the city of Boston was a warzone, and it was difficult to avoid this never ending stream of violence. As a juvenile I ran amok and did a few stints in DYS (Department of Youth Services). However, the worst was yet to come.

Eventually I graduated to more serious, or should I say, the older I got the more serious the crimes got. Selling drugs, doing stick-ups, and running with a crew that did not care about anything, became a part of my everyday existence.

Throughout all of this fast living, and hard running, I had a child at the age of sixteen. I thought I knew what it was to be a father, but in reality, I was far from being mature enough. By having a child you would think I would fly the straight and narrow and start being responsible. Negative.

I allowed myself to continue living a life that eventually led to me swapping my freedom for a prison cell. In 1991 I was charged with murder. I stayed on the run for a couple of years until 1993. In 1994, I was convicted and sentenced to life in prison.

In prison, I got involved with all the negativity that comes with a "survival of the fittest" environment. I was robbing dudes, fighting with the CO's, and just wilding out. This is how I chose to deal with my incarceration. I was hopeless. I felt as if life did not matter anymore.

In April of 1996, I was sent to the DDU, (Departmental Disciplinary Unit), the notorious "prison within a prison" in the Massachusetts correctional system. For ten years straight I sat in the DDU, and this is where I began my personal transformation.

It did not happen overnight. I was still at war with the evil forces of uncertainty and vice. I found refuge in reading and educating myself, things that I never believed in because I never had a clear example as to what would come from it.

I started to realize that a lot of aspects of life were bigger than me, and began to stop feeling sorry for myself. I initiated a change in my mental condition by fully embracing the faith of Islam. I then addressed my emotional condition, and soon began to understand that a man does not make excuses, he makes progress.

The late Nelson Mandela once said, "When a man is denied the right to live the life he believes in, he has no choice but to become an outlaw." I am not saying that someone denied me the right to live the life I believed in, I denied MYSELF the right to live the life I was SUPPOSED to live.

There were no boundaries for me; no guardrails to deter my spiral into this human meat locker. When you are a teenager, coming up fast the way I and so many others like me have come up, your mind does not have the ability to process your sense of self-control. As a man who was once a child raised in the streets and in prison, I know better now than I knew then, and pray that no one else's child has to succumb to life in a cell.

-*Zachariah Ibrahim-Bush, Man of Fortitude and Peace*

In order to get to the present, you have to begin in the past. My birth name is Jeffrey Anthony. I was born at Boston Medical Center on February 21, 1978. I grew up in the Greater Boston area for the most part, until my family decided to move around a bit. We lived in Dorchester, Everett, and Chelsea, places that would define my youth.

My parents are both from Antigua, and they tried their hardest to raise my three brothers, my two sisters and me. When I was eight years old, my father decided to disappear, leaving my mother to raise six kids. I believe this had a negative effect on me because I was too young to understand my mother's tears.

At age eleven, a relative came from New York came to visit, and that is when my life changed. He introduced me to gang life, and being that he was the only assertive, confident older male that I had in my life, I dove headfirst into a game that a lot of us so effortlessly play.

Being so young and witnessing things that I could not understand, I accepted my role as a soldier who was willing to sacrifice it all. I started hustling full time, and by the time I was sixteen, I became a full-fledged member of the gang.

I put forth all of my efforts to achieve rank in the gang. I was going so hard and so fast, that at age twenty, me and three relatives were arrested for murder in the first degree. The reality of my bad decision making had finally ruined not only my life, but the lives of so many others.

While awaiting trial, I had a lot of time to reflect on life, myself, and all the people that I hurt, and finally came to the realization that the life I was living was crazy and wanted something different. I had lost too much trying to be a man, because I had no idea what a man was.

-*Jeffrey Anthony, Man of Reflection*

From the Outside

Not every voice that needs to be heard has to be from behind the wall. There are people in our society who are victims to the criminal justice system that have to endure stigmatization and the perpetual status of "criminal".

Even when a person fights for what is right, in a civil way, or stands up for themselves, they are subject to punishment. It is no wonder that there is a disconnection between people. It is no wonder that in certain communities and in certain circumstances, in regards to the law, distrust is stronger than trust.

I think the criminal justice system is horrible. I have been through it from both ends. First asking for help, then at the receiving end of "justice".

I was in an abusive relationship for a long time, which resulted in physical violence. I was arrested and placed in a holding cell for three days at a local police station, (Monday was a holiday). I had no access to a phone, nor did I have any bail. I have three children, and I could not speak to them and at least tell them that I was alive. As a mother, it hurt my heart. As a female, where do I begin to explain how my dignity was affected by being locked up?

I was stripped naked, searched, and ridiculed by both male and female police officers for no apparent reason. The cell I was placed in was freezing cold. No blanket, no toilet paper, no soap. The sink was a toilet. Hours later, they put another female prisoner in the cell with me who was clearly intoxicated. She screamed all night.

Other female prisoners in different cells were begging the police officers to take them to the hospital. I felt so helpless and lost, that I really did not know how I would get through this. When the day came for me to go to court, (Tuesday), I was not allowed to shower, brush my teeth, or even comb my hair. I will be the first to tell you I smelled terrible, and I felt even worse.

What had I put my kids through? I knew that my children were heartbroken, afraid, and confused, and I knew that I would have to make things right. First, I had to deal with my case.

By the grace and mercy of God, my case was dismissed and eventually closed. However, I was referred to the Department of Children and Families, (DCF). They stayed in my life for two years even after my case was resolved, "investigating the welfare of my children".

I felt as if I had no control over my family or myself. The worst part is, when I did try to get my life back on track, the CORI prevented me from getting a decent job. To this day, even though I was never convicted of a crime, my CORI has made it more difficult to get housing, and even food for my children. Yes, food. I had to reapply for SNAP benefits three times before I was eligible, and the question they continued to bring up was, "Well, what about this case?" It is almost as if I will be looked at as a criminal for the rest of my life.

-Debbie R., Mother, Survivor

I have given the Commonwealth of Massachusetts 10 and a half years of my life. The first time I fell into the cycle of constantly dealing with law enforcement, I was 18 years a fool. Strong, intelligent, and angry with no sense of direction, the streets of Boston gave me my purpose.

Since then, I have learned that a high percentage of people caught up in the criminal justice system come from families and communities that are far from perfect. With schools that are underfunded and neighborhoods that are havens of crime, yet and still, people like myself and others try to find ways to cope.

What we saw around us forced us to want more, yet without true guidance, a life of trying to get over filled the voids on our side of town. In no way do I write these words to try and justify crime, I am just stating the truth. It is not difficult to pick up a package of drugs or a pistol when these things are always, readily available. Not some times, not just on Monday and Wednesday, but ALWAYS.

To see my hardworking family struggle just to scrape out a living did something to me that made me bitter towards the world in which I lived. I did not feel as if someone owed me something, rather I felt as if I owed my family something better than what we had, and I was determined to go after it.

I chased what I believed was a way out. In actuality, it was a way into a system that has broken the will of many, and will continue to do so until we as people strive to make it better, or destroy it altogether.

- *Alex Jeanty, Soldier of Integrity*

Prisoners of conscience: defined by Amnesty International as: "people who have been jailed because of their political beliefs ...provided they have neither used nor advocated violence."

During the 1960s and 1970s a growing number of peace organizations sponsored demonstrations against the Vietnam War. In the late 1960s I traveled to a large protest in Washington DC on a chartered bus with members of the War Resister's League. When we arrived in DC we stored our sleeping bags in a church hall already filled with sleeping bags. We would sleep there that night.

For me the highlight of the day's events was an action at the White House. Several dozen of us had decided to commit civil disobedience there to mourn the napalming of innocent civilians and to demand an end to the decades-long war. When we occupied an area we were not permitted to enter, we were arrested. At the jail we were given two choices: (a) plead guilty, pay a fine, and be released or (b) plead not-guilty and be locked up. I was one of the handful of people who refused to pay the fine. Along with six other resisters, I was imprisoned.

We were prisoners of conscience. We were using our right of free speech to criticize the power elite and to influence governmental policies. To some degree the DC prison system recognized that we were different from most other prisoners. We were placed in a block of cells separate from the general prison population. Only in the cafeteria at mealtimes did we encounter other inmates.

Although our cells were set apart, we were processed in the standard way. We were taken to a bare room with a cement floor and required to strip. Then we were hosed down, and our bodies were examined. We were given prison garments to put on, and we were locked into our cells to await trial.

What I remember most vividly about this process was feeling powerless. From one minute to the next, I no longer had any control over my life. I was absolutely at the mercy of a hostile system that perceived me as a menace to law and order.

My detention was short. The next morning our case was heard in court and the Judge dismissed the charges. We were released later that day, but I was marked for life. The loss of freedom had been an overwhelming experience. Although I was incarcerated for only 24 hours, my world view had changed. Although I had only a partial experience of the prison culture because our cells were set apart, I felt a sense of doom I have never forgotten.

As an adult I had always been concerned about the abusive treatment of offenders. I had empathized especially with the misery of people who were unjustly accused or given long prison sentences for minor offenses. But now I had a personal experience of the machinery of the penal system. I felt my powerlessness in a system that was set up to dehumanize offenders.

-Bill Himelhoch, Social Servant, Man of Conscience

"Ready, Set, Release"

Nelson Mandela was quoted after serving 27 years in prison on Robben Island that, "I learned that courage isn't the absence of fear, but the courage to triumph over it."

Over the past year and half that I have had the awesome privilege of being the Executive Director of New Start Project in which our mission is reducing recidivism by advocating and supporting the successful reintegration of men and women returning from incarceration. I have worked with men and women returning from incarceration and I have learned that the re-entry journey back into society from incarceration requires unbelievable courage and determination. For many, there is no pre-release preparation that can prepare a person for the moment they are released and escorted through the last gate of an institution. The burden of the responsibility of having to pick up where one left off; and being placed under enormous expectations to succeed with many having no resources or less than before being incarcerated.

Many re-entry residents experience gate fever, which is an overwhelming sense of nervousness and anxiety that one feels while being released. The nervousness experienced is like one standing at the starting line of an Olympic track tournament and hears "Ready, Set, Go!" For re-entry residents, they experience "Ready, Set, Release!" Once released men and women have to run at a volatile and rapid pace to prove themselves, demonstrate progress, and to show that they have learned their lesson for the crimes that they have committed. The responsibilities of probation fees, parole, child support, housing, employment, rebuilding family relationships, and managing personal struggles like addiction.

Unfortunately, many are not prepared and conditioned to meet these expectations and overcome the personal and systematic barriers that they must face after release. As an advocate of re-entry residents, I am convinced that the immediate obstacle to re-entry success is personal not systematic.

Rebuilding and starting over begins with self! Singing legend Michael Jackson recorded a song entitled "Man in the Mirror". A verse in this song declares, "I'm starting with the man in the mirror. If you want to make the world a better place, take a look at yourself and then make the change." This is powerful because in order for us to change the systems that create barriers we have to create a personal environment that cultivates potential that empowers individuals to change systematic barriers.

All men and women returning from prison have personal barriers that they must overcome. Some have been released for a few months to five years. In order for them to get to the finish line of successful re-entry, they must overcome obstacles such as: self-doubt, low self-esteem, addiction, loneliness, emotional trauma, anger, threats of violence, and toxic relationships.

In May of 2014, New Start Project participated in a Criminal Offender Record Information Job Fair. I remember a young man who visited our career table while we were conducting pre-screening interviews. Part of the interview process was to have people invent a product that would solve any problem that they had in their life and convince me to buy the product. This particular young man was nervous and told me he couldn't conduct the pre-screen interview because he hadn't prepared and needed time to gather his thoughts.

I immediately responded with, "Okay, I understand." However, I realized that it was a mistake and then challenged the young man to try. I told him that I would help him get through it. He reluctantly agreed. After he took my computer keyboard and created a job creation machine, he gave the most articulate and passionate case for his product. I realized that people returning from incarceration are under a lot of pressure and that pressure creates fear and anxiety. They must have a safe place and community support to be successful.

In the ancient scriptures the divine declared, "Behold I will do a new thing; now it shall spring forth; shall ye not know it? I will even make a way in the wilderness, and rivers in the deserts." As a community, it is our civic duty to work alongside those returning home and create opportunities and resources for our fellow citizens.

There are over 5 billion people on the planet and each one of us is special, significant, and full of potential. Potential is the release of one's full ability. Despite our pasts, we have the capability to tap into our gifts and talents. In every person who has been incarcerated there is potential. For every ex-prisoner there is an entrepreneur, inventor, organizational leader, community leader, spiritual leader, parent, husband, wife, homeowner, and a prosperous individual. Despite having a criminal record we all share the responsibility to release our potential.

Sometimes society forgets that re-entry residents are people too. Re-entry Residents didn't wake up one day and say, I want to be incarcerated, marginalized, and stigmatized. Re-entry Residents are people who are filled with dreams and ideas, (untapped potential), that can change a world that is yearning for pathways to navigate through the wilderness of injustice, inequality, violence, racism, hunger and disease.

So with that being said, this leads me to pose a question, what does it take to successfully reintegrate from incarceration? From incarceration to release there is a between. Between implies a process, a process from one destination to another. 95% of all prisoners are between the process of serving time and re-entry. At New Start Project we have 6 core values: Community, Accountability, Responsibility, Equality Opportunity, Relationship Building, and Social Entrepreneurship.

Our first value is community, which is critical to successful re-entry. The community gives us a stage to demonstrate our other values. Community allows us to have daily human transactions in a potential safe space where relationships are formed and cultivated. It is an environment where individuals can demonstrate our ability to be accountable and responsible. The community as a whole can work collectively to create a culture of equal opportunity and create socioeconomic opportunities that lead to safety and prosperity. For example, community organizations provide job training, education, housing, medical care, mental health, substance abuse treatment, pro bono legal consultation, and family re-unification services for re-entry residents.

Communities that are united and prosperous empower every member in the community and encourages personal responsibility. When a community is on one accord and share certain values, they experience prosperity which can be transformed into power and influence that helps develop leaders, including re-entry residents. Re-entry leaders can take the leadership role in breaking down systematic barriers that help contribute to the 50% recidivism rate in in the state of Massachusetts. Many of these systematic barriers are erected in the form of laws and policies. The Registered Motor Vehicle License Restriction bill is a great example. The law is an existential barrier that re-entry advocates are fighting to tear down in the state of Massachusetts.

The RMV restriction bill currently suspends the license of any person convicted of a drug offense for five years and requires a reinstatement fee of up to $500. Currently in the state of Massachusetts, of the 7,000 people who have their licenses suspended under this law annually, only 2,500 people get their license reinstated. I know several re-entry residents who cannot obtain a driver's license, including one of New Start Project's board members.

Brendan has been out of prison for four years, and in July, we celebrated his fourth year of sobriety. Brendan is the epitome of New Start Project values and he has demonstrated an unshakeable commitment to building community relationships. Brendan is the current senior supervisor for a public charity.

The organization raises funds on behalf of Non-Profit organizations such as the Red Cross and Children's International Fund. His job requires him to be mobile and do daily site visits with his staff. He cannot rent a car, cannot accept supervisor promotions in other locations because of his inability to travel. His sole means of travel is public transportation. Brendan has raised millions of dollars for charities, he has served faithfully on our board of directors, and he has rebuilt his relationship with his family, and proven to be a committed and reliable partner in an intimate relationship. For others the situation is bleaker.

We have members of NSP who cannot afford to pay their driver's license reinstatement fee or purchase a state ID. Almost 70% do not have a proper ID, and it becomes an impediment to securing employment and to fully reintegrate into society.

Re-entry residents have no choice but to reintegrate back into the community. The other option is to go back, and going back may provide temporary shelter and structure, but makes it more difficult to reunite families, provide economic security for our children, and become social entrepreneurs that cultivate relationships and networking.

From my experience, the re-entry community is very familiar with overcoming the odds in the pursuit of freedom and a better life. Harriet Tubman, an African American woman who was the Moses of the Underground Railroad, led slaves between the deserts of slavery of the south to the streams of freedom in the north. As they journeyed between slavery to freedom, Harriet Tubman gave the slaves some great advice. If you hear the dogs barking, keep going. If you see the fire torches, keep going. If you hear them shouting stop, keep going!

As a man of faith I have to put my faith into action and get going! So that we the community can work collectively with those who are between the bars and headed out of the gates. Providing re-entry residents with the opportunity to live a fulfilling life beyond bars will hopefully lead to their children and grandchildren to avoid prison, poverty, being a high school dropout, living in dilapidated housing, a victim of substance addiction, and mental illness. In exchange for our collective investment in the release of men and women returning from incarceration, we will have generations of college graduates, an expansive middle class that includes: housing developers, substance abuse counselors, community leaders and responsible leaders of their family.

Re-entry barriers are the great gulf between the American dream and our current reality for the millions who have returned from incarceration. Will we turn the other cheek and look the other way? Or will we be like the divine in the ancient scriptures that made paths in the wilderness and streams in the desert! Between and beyond the bars is hope, freedom and victory, and with the divine's help, our journey is unknown, yet our outcome is certain. There has always been a great struggle between justice and cruelty, freedom and bondage, and we know that God is not neutral between them. For every re-entry resident I declare, Ready, Set, Go! Go and be bold, and don't be afraid or discouraged, for vision, hope, and opportunity are with you everywhere you go.

-Tony Smith, Director, New Start Project

<u>CHAPTER 3</u>

<u>RACISM</u>

A History of Racism

Secrets are dangerous. This country of ours has many secrets when it comes to race and race relations. Some may argue that the times in which we now live are different than they were fifty years ago, that the advancement of several minority groups, black people in particular, has erased the struggle that comes with change. I stand here to fuss that they are not. The clock is broken and has not moved forward.

When laws are ratified to maintain order and law enforcement is given the authority to uphold this order, then what *order* is it that is being maintained and upheld? Is it the order that refused to indict the murderers of a simple man like Eric Garner a few months ago? Or is it the same order that acquitted J.W. Milam and Roy Bryant in less than an hour for kidnapping and brutally killing Emmett Till in 1955? (For the record, Milam and Bryant, who were both white, both confessed to Till's murder in a magazine article a year later. Incredibly, they were never indicted. Even more incredible: they were paid $4,000 for contributing to the article.)

When the incomparable Dr. Martin Luther King Jr. delivered his passionate "I Have A Dream" speech on August the 28th in 1963, racist white folks were relieved that he was only having a dream. They said, "You keep right on dreaming while we send our children to college; while our children become senators and state representatives; while we send white men into outer space and plant the flag of the United States on the Moon."

This racist mindset, this syndrome, did not magically vanish with the passage of time. Rather it became immersed into the social systems, structures, and institutions that are still at the helm of this country.

When we consider the fact that the Civil Rights Movement earnestly tried to sustain a non-violent approach, it was still met with the destructive forces of a racist, white power structure. This power structure mandated that it was well within the guidelines of the law for a sheriff and his deputies to turn attack dogs on black women and children. The "Hands Up, Don't Shoot" mantra of today is just the echo of "We Shall Overcome" from half a century ago.

We can be certain that the discriminatory practices of fifty years ago are still alive and well. Not only because the theory of racial inequality is embedded in the majority of social institutions across this country, but because, what *really* has been done to destroy the system of racism? Systems do not disappear simply with the passage of time. Time heals, but it does not destroy. The people who forge these systems pass on, however, their legacy remains.

Sociologist par excellence, Dr. Madeline Cousineau, says in her phenomenal work, "Introducing Sociology: A Whole New World", that some social problems call for more than just acknowledging them. She states:

"When problems in society are institutional, they are difficult to change, and solutions must go beyond help for the individual. This is the nature of racism in our society"

A system has to be destroyed or else it will resurface and function under a new name or "-ism". Slavery, Jim Crow, the Black Codes, "subprime" loans, President Obama being depicted on a food stamp, "welfare queen", "crack baby"; these are just a few off the long list of derogatory and disrespectful phrases and incidences that have become attached to black people as a race.

Walter Mosley, one of the most prolific storytellers and architects of the written word the world has ever seen, touches on the point of racial inequality in his essay entitled, "Workin' On the Chain Gang." In reference to black life after slavery, he states:

"With no history other than slavery and no future because the white world blocked the way, black people never bought the

American dream-at least not completely, at least not for long. The story of the history between blacks and whites was punctuated with lynchings and random violence. The accepted dialogue between the races was a partial return to the master-slave dynamic."

Centuries after "plantation" slavery, what are the fundamental differences between race relations in this country? Being free and being equal are two different arteries. Equality means that you can speak your mind and say things for what they are. No gloss. No color. Just the truth. The heavy burden of establishing one's self comes with freedom. Justice, that long sought after elixir of the oppressed, comes with equality.

Black folks have long since been on the waiting list for equality in America. We have always been told: "Calm down Negroes! We will eventually get around to giving you full justice, but first, let us drop some justice on Japan, let us inject some democracy in Vietnam, and let us shoot some patriotism into Iraq and Afghanistan!" People of color, citizens of the United States, have always been forced to be on standby while the

American government worries about injustice across the oceans.

Even now, we as black people are made to appear as if we have no right to voice our complaints. As if the atrocious acts committed against Medgar Evers, Sean Bell, Emmitt Till, Abner Louima, James Byrd, Trayvon Martin, Michael Brown, and Eric Garner can be forgotten because Massachusetts had a black governor. What about those four precious black girls, Cynthia Wesley, Carole Robertson, Addie Mae Collins, and Denise McNair, who were burned to death in a church down in Alabama? Are we to forget about that overt racism because two other girls from Alabama grew up to become Oprah Winfrey and Condoleezza Rice? Shortly after Dr. Martin Luther King Jr. said that he had a dream in which he envisioned black children holding hands with white children, he was foully murdered. Does this fact get swept away and forgotten because Barack Obama is President of the United States? Absolutely not.

When black folks appear to be too passionate about a social issue that has far-

Leonard Swafford-Donald

reaching implications, and they have some semblance of influence, they are either murdered, discredited, or, all of a sudden, everyone wants to *talk,* simple and plain. It is amazing how the burden of dialogue and being reasonable is placed on the shoulders of black folks. When we are attacked-physically, politically, socially, economically, and spiritually (racism is spirit murder),-by the most unreasonable and unapologetic forces of terrorism the world has ever seen, no one wants to talk until we bite back.

Bear in mind that the social upheavals in Ferguson and other cities across the country, are just reverberations of Watts in 1965, Detroit in 1967, Newark in 1967, and Los Angeles in 1992. All of these incidences resulted in military intervention. All of these incidences held race and race relations as the driving force that catapulted the issue of inequality back into America's face.

When the Transatlantic Slave Trade morphed into blatant racism against people of color, black people began to realize that they would have to fight for their lives, for the rest of their lives. There was no break in the battle, no respite from the reaper of white supremacy. With this fight came a hardening of hearts, which made it easy for the fiery, backwoods preacher Nat Turner to kill women and children. It made it relevant for the Nation of Islam founder Elijah Muhammad to refer to white folks as "devils". These mindsets were the results of having one's humanness ground into gristle, the hate that hate produced.

Disagreement is the bride of malfunction. There is no melody to racism. It vehemently stands opposed to everything that this country *claims* it stands for. Until we as a people fortify an orchestrated effort to confront and combat issues of race, we will never have a society that all people will look forward to contributing to.

The Legend of Clocletz

According to slave legend, a phantom Indian chief who roamed the swamps in the South at night was named "Clocletz".

The real "Clocletz" were a historical Indian tribe that showed indifference toward black slaves, and were oftentimes employed as slave hunters.

In June, 1866, six Confederate veterans of the Civil War formed the first chapter of the Ku Klux Klan in Pulaski, Tennessee. A Confederate general named Nathan Bedford Forrest was installed as the "Grand Wizard", one of the highest "honors" the Klan could bestow upon its members. In adopting the name "Ku Klux", (a play on the aforementioned word "Clocletz"), it instilled fear in its intended victims: black people.

At its core, the Ku Klux Klan was a white, fundamentalist, terrorist organization that employed acts of torture ranging from rape to lynchings to hobble the progress of black people on their road to equality.

Referring to themselves as "the Invisible Empire", because their influence and reach permeated throughout most aspects of Southern society, the Klan's membership swelled to the tens of thousands within a span of five years of its formation. Judges, sheriffs, merchants, preachers, and politicians-people considered well-to-do, upstanding citizens-joined the Ku Klux Klan.

Having chapters throughout the South with many names, (Pale Faces, Knights of the Rising Sun, '76 Association, Knights of the White Camellia, Constitutional Union Guards, Council of Safety), the Klan openly engaged in wholesale murder.

Murder is a vicious crime, even more so when the motivating factor is race. When you claim to despise someone based on their race and ethnicity, I have to ask: What monster created the world that you live in?

I ask this so that the activities and doctrines of the Ku Klux Klan are kept in their proper place. Prejudice is a thought. Discrimination is an action. Racism is a syndrome. Therefore, acts of racism, are psychological disturbances that have no place in our society.

In April, 1871, the U.S. Congress passed the Third Enforcement Act, also known as the Ku Klux Klan Act. This bill of legislature called Klan activity an act of rebellion against the U.S. government. Section 1 of this act became Section 1983, which states:

"Every person who, under color of any statute, ordinance, regulation, custom, or usage, of any State or Territory or the District of Columbia, subjects or causes to be subjected, any citizen of the United States or other person within the jurisdiction thereof to the deprivation of any rights, privileges, or immunities secured by the Constitution and laws, shall be liable to the party injured in an action at law, suit in equity, or other proper proceeding for redress..."

Section 1983 does not mention race, and it is applicable to people of any color, but it was *originally* passed specifically to help black people enforce the new constitutional rights that were won after the Civil War specifically, the 13th, 14th, and 15th Amendments to the U.S. Constitution.

These amendments made slavery illegal, established the right to "due process of law", equal protection of the laws, and guaranteed every male citizen the right to vote.

The Klan knew that if a black man was recognized as free, he would be recognized as a citizen, thus, he would gain the right to vote. This led the "Invisible Empire" to terrorize potential black voters before they even reached the polls. Also, soon after Section 1983 became law, Northern businessmen joined forces with Southern plantation owners to take back the limited freedom that black people had won. Federal judges found excuses to undermine Section 1983 along with most of the other civil rights bills passed by Congress.

Although the purpose of Section 1983 was to bypass the racist state courts, federal judges ruled that most lawsuits had to go back to those same state courts. Their rulings remained law until black people began to regain their political strength through the numerous movements for civil and human rights in the 1960's.

As far as the Ku Klux Klan is concerned, their legacy, and most certainly the entity itself, is still alive and functioning. Under the guise of political organizations, fraternal orders, corporate businesses, and social clubs, the policies that foster black inferiority is no myth or legend. Dear Reader, for all intents and purposes, the "Legend of Clocletz" is a reality.

CHAPTER 4

RESOURCES AND FINANCIAL OPPORTUNITY

A PENNY SAVED

I am pretty sure that my readers are familiar with the old adage, "a penny saved is a penny earned". This saying is based on the notion that, by saving enough pennies, they will eventually become rolls of quarters, and these, in turn, will become dollars. Economic growth, on a minute scale, from coin to paper.

We are currently experiencing one of the worst economic downturns this nation has ever faced in the last century. Initially, legislators and policymakers, split by party affiliation and special interests, made an indolent approach in regards to this financial bogeyman. It was not until the major financial institutions of this nation started to show their fallibility that the brigadiers of Capitol Hill saddled up and declared war on the economic crisis.

Prior to this whirlwind of financial chaos, this country was already in a ten trillion dollar, (count that on your fingers), national budget deficit. Thirty-three million Americans had already lived below the poverty line, and of this lurid number, roughly, nine million are African –American, non-English speaking, or have some form of disability.

Everyone who cannot make a car payment, buy food for their children, or get a prescription filled for much needed medicine because their health insurance does not cover it, needs to ask this question to anyone who cares to listen: Who did the federal government really bail out with the economic stimulus package? 700 billion dollars was just the tip of the iceberg. By passing the bill, the council on "The Hill" only put out the fire, they did not rebuild Rome.

I am no economy expert, by far, but neither am I so disillusioned to think that everyone who was already on the lower rung of the socioeconomic ladder were somehow rescued by the passage of the aforementioned bill. The bailout was only intended to stabilize the credit market, not fix it. Consequently, even with the credit market stabilized, what does this exactly imply? Will this new line of credit help everyone, or just the few who spit in the wind in the first place?

Will this credit be extended to the local Boys and Girls Club to help build a new computer wing? This not only helps our kids, it also opens up jobs for laborers, contractors, and youth counselors. Will the credit find its way to the mom and pop convenience store that has served the community for decades, and desperately needs a loan to refinance their property? Or, will this credit make it to the grandmother who is raising her children's children, but who cannot afford to buy them food for their stomachs, clothes for school, and hygiene and medicinal products for their well-being?

If saving the economy was as easy as printing more currency, I am certain that the U.S. Treasury would do just that. Unfortunately, the problem with making "fresh dollars" is as such: when the economy is flooded with "new" money, especially on a nationwide level, it undermines the currency that is already in circulation. It weakens the economic marrow of any nation, even more so if the nation operates on a capitalist/consumer wavelength like ours.

Here is another example: the U.S. dollar is at its strongest when there is just enough to sustain our economy, no more, no less. What this essentially means is that when the least amount of U.S. currency flows from the hands of the average American through major businesses and federally insured banks, and then trickles back to the American citizen, it maintains its value. When this same currency is taken from our nation and filtered through international banks and foreign financial markets, its stock and demand rises, thus, its value increases.

Because the U.S. and a handful of other countries can back up its capital (money), with various assets, liquid or otherwise, and goods, the foreign exchange rate is overwhelming.

Countries with weak economies that lack the resources to support the value of their currency, try to entice American investors by displaying carnivals of financial opportunity in order to get the U.S. dollar flowing through their economic veins. When this happens, the U.S. dollar is crowned the sovereign monarch of the *Third World's* economy and there is no need to print more money. Less is more, at least in the sense of value.

How did our dollars fail and become devalued? Well, as simple as I can place it, here is how. The less is more philosophy has always been adhered to, with the exception that it was altered in such a manner that the flop of our economy was inevitable. Single, obtrusively wealthy institutions wanted more money, and in their intrepid pursuit, *less* of the money was actually making its way back into the economy, back into the hands of the people.

Imagine a game of Monopoly[2], in which I take all of the money and property and "break the bank". What happens next? There is no way for the other players to continue unless I allow them back into the game in the form of a loan or credit (sound familiar?).

---

[2] Monopoly is a registered trademark of Parker Bros, LLC

Either that, or, we start the game over from scratch, and we all begin with the same amount of money, (wouldn't that be noble in the real world?). Certain CEO's and CFO's of certain financial institutions, "broke the bank', so to speak, and the other players-the people and the economy-had no way to continue playing the game. Undoubtedly, this chain of events did not happen in a femtosecond, just as a game of Monopoly does not climax for hours, maybe even days.

The question then remains, what us gon' do now? First of all, get involved. Beat on the door of your local Congress people and demand to know. Solid questions should extract solid answers. We tend to forget that our votes, the ones that placed our elected officials into their plush, corner offices, really count. Take a proactive stance. Make a phone call, write a letter, or send an e-mail. Find out!

I want my readers to bear in mind this fact: if it were you or I engaging in such blatant acts of greed like those wolfish financial institutions at the expense of so many, the guillotine would be well oiled, and the executioner would have surely been whistling that dreadful tune. Save your pennies, spite the executioner.

CHAPTER 5

EDUCATION

.

"A university should be a place of light, liberty, and of learning."
-Benjamin Disraeli

PERFORMANCE-BASED FUNDING: CHASING OUTCOMES OVER REAL LEARNING

Performance funding for public colleges and universities is a bad idea on fire these days. Even as more research clearly shows the plans do not work as intended, nearly 30 states, most recently Florida, have adopted punitive approaches to paying for higher education.

"They have this one-size-fits-all vision for higher education, and they have one idea about what a model university should be," said Tom Auxter, president of the United Faculty of Florida. "They don't get that different universities have different missions, and different constituencies that they serve."

Twenty-five states currently have some kind of performance-based funding system for their public <u>colleges and universities,</u> and five (Colorado, Georgia, Montana, South Dakota and Virginia) have approved plans not fully in place yet, according to the National Conference of State Legislatures.

The way performance-based funding typically works is a state will set aside 5 to 50 percent of their higher-ed funding, and then use those millions of dollars to reward institutions with the most graduates or course completers. Although NCSL encourages states to also "reward colleges that graduate low-income, minority and adult students to ensure that institutions keep serving these populations," most states do not have benchmarks that acknowledge some students take longer to graduate or may need additional support along the way.

In Florida specifically, the new plan prioritizes the percentage of graduates with <u>jobs</u>; the average wages of graduates; the cost per degree; the six-year graduation rate; the number of STEM degrees; the percentage of students with <u>Pell Grants</u>, and a few other factors. The three (out of nine) universities that perform worst according to these metrics will lose probably 1 percent of their funding this year-or about $200,000 a year, under pending legislation-while the other six get more money.

All of these new plans replace traditional formulas, which financed institutions according to how many students they served, and how many faculty, staff, and other resources they needed to deliver a high-quality education. But those traditional formulas are expensive, and anyway, states have not fully funded education in a long, long time.

Where's the Money?

"(State legislators) are evading the question, and the question is: what does it take to adequately fund our <u>community colleges</u>?" said Joe LeBlanc, president of the Massachusetts Community College Council. In Massachusetts, up to 50 percent of state funding for two-year colleges now depends on graduation rates and other metrics.

Meanwhile, funding for Massachusetts higher education plummeted 38 percent between 2008 and 2012. "We're not even close to fully funded," LeBlanc scoffed.

Not surprisingly, Florida is right there, too, with a 41 percent cut over the past four years. And they are not even the worst. During those same years, funding to higher education was chopped by half in Arizona and New Hampshire. Making matters worse, those cuts have come on top of decades of previous cuts. As a result, public colleges in the U.S. have essentially become privatized. At the University of Oregon, for example, just 5 percent of the school's operating costs will be covered by the state this year.

"To work, even in theory, performance-based funding depends on rewarding the most successful, so it depends on more funding," said Mark F. Smith, NEA senior policy analyst for higher education. "But there are much better investments for that additional funding that would actually help students learn," he pointed out. (Academic counseling, for example, has been shown to increase student persistence and graduation rates.)

And it Doesn't Even Work

If the aim of performance-based funding is to elicit more college graduates-something the United States needs in the multi-millions to keep up with its workforce demands-then we should see increasing graduation rates in states with those plans, yes?

The answer is no, according to several studies, including one by David Tandberg of Florida State University. In a co-authored paper, "State Performance Funding for Higher Education: Silver Bullet or Red Herring?" Tandberg found that performance funding "more often than not" failed to effect degree completion.

In fact, in the few instances where it did have an effect, *it was more likely to be negative;* graduation rates actually declined. The authors concluded: "Our analyses revealed that performance funding is not the silver bullet some are making it out to be. Instead, it may be a red herring, distracting policymakers from dealing with more fundamental policy problems, such as inadequate state funding or student financial aid."

Meanwhile, another study shows the effects of performance-funding might be particularly harmful at historically black colleges and universities (HBCUs), where often students take more time to graduate because they are also working or taking additional developmental courses.

The unintended consequences of outcomes-based funding plans have been made very clear in K12 education, where big rewards for high-stakes reading and math test scores have led schools to set aside other subjects, like science and art. But unintended does not mean unanticipated-in the 2011 NEA Thought & Action journal, Diane Ravitch warned higher-ed faculty and staff about the likely consequences of chasing "outcomes" for funding.

"This is the pursuit of numbers for the sake of meeting a quota, not for the sake of learning," she said. "If numbers are our goal, we can give every student a college degree and not subject them to the trouble (and expense) of going to classes. In fact, with the rapid spread of online 'learning', that seems to be the wave of the future."

There is also the cautionary tale of the Soviet shoes, often recounted by Richard Rothstein of the Economic Policy Institute. To meet impossibly high Kremlin quotas for shoes, Soviet factory workers just made smaller shoes!

Unfortunately, they did not fit anyone. - *Mary Ellen Flannery, National Education Association*

CHAPTER 6

STRUCTURAL PROBLEMS WITHIN FAMILIES

CHILD ABUSE

Abuse is defined as treatment in a harmful, injurious or offensive way; to speak insultingly, harshly, and unjustly to or about; to use wrongly or improperly; and to neglect[3]. Abuse occurs every day, everywhere in some way, shape or form. When it comes to children, the most common forms of abuse are neglect, physical and emotional.

In order to achieve accurate statistics of the number of abuse cases in the U.S., everyone must do their part in reporting suspicions of abuse and neglect to protect our young citizens. However, many people do not, and most suspicions of abuse are reported by teachers and physicians. Studies show that a report of child abuse is made every ten seconds and more than four

---

[3] www.dictionary.com

children die each day as a result of child abuse.[4]

There are several warning signs that a child is being neglected and abused, but children are defenseless against such brutality when they are too young to understand why they are being treated in such a negative manner. Therefore, it is up to anyone who witnesses such heinous treatment to act on behalf of the child, (or children's') safety and report abusive incidents.

In 2011, neglect was the highest ranked type of abuse with over 500,000 incidents reported, and physical abuse as the runner up with just over 100,000 incidents reported.[5] Neglect is defined as paying too little or no attention to; disregard or showing negligence.[6]

Child abuse is a vicious cycle that begins to occur most often before the age of four. Most children who are abused will grow up

---

[4] http://www.childhelp-usa.com/pages/statistics

[5] http://www.childhelp-usa.com/pages/statistics

[6] www.dictionary.com

to abuse their own children and approximately 80% of 21 year olds who were abused as children met the requirements for having at least one psychological disorder as reported in 2011.[7] About 25% of abused children will experience teen pregnancy, and abused teens are more likely to engage in sexual risk taking. With these facts alone, one can clearly see why child abuse is not only a continuous cycle, but a destructive one.

One of the most profound issues in parenting is lack of positive attention given to children. A teen parent who was abused and neglected as a child is much more likely to be an abusive and neglectful parent, simply because they were raised in such an environment where they were improperly treated and do not know any other way to treat their own children. They are also more prone to be neglectful because they were not able to experience their adolescent years as they should have; developing positive relationships, thus resulting in the child or children being left with family, friends, or even alone so that the teen parent can hang

---

[7] http://www.childhelp-usa.com/pages/statistics

out and socialize as they would have normally done had they not been a parent.

Research shows that some parents feel trapped and burdened by their children because they cannot live the life they want to live, and this leads to an inner anger that is released on the child whether it be in the form of hitting, yelling, or far worse actions. These types of actions result in emotional trauma to the child and being defenseless as they are, they do not know what to do in order for the abuse to stop.

Even if old enough to speak, children are afraid to tell someone if they are constantly being hit for many reasons.

First, a child is not able to recognize abuse and be able to describe it as such and will feel as though they are being punished for something they did wrong, though that is far from the case. Second, if a child confides in another adult, family member or friend, it will eventually come back to their parent, and one time is all it takes for an embittered, unfit parent to be confronted to turn it back on the child and abuse them even worse for speaking on the matter. This leaves the child afraid to ever speak up again. Thirdly, a child cannot fully explain their feelings, and due to being abused, they will act out to receive the attention they are not getting at home.

About 50-60% of child fatalities due to abuse and neglect are reported to be due to such causes on death certificates. The frighteningly sad concept about the preceding statement is that if this many deaths are being shown as statistically accurate, why are they not being reported properly on death certificates so the perpetrators may be subject to legal action?

Physical abuse is the next leading type of maltreatment among children. Physical abuse consists of excessive physical force against a child whether it be hitting with hands, other body parts or objects. Physical abuse is most commonly reported by professionals, most of which are teachers who see the abuse victim on a regular basis. Although teachers are typically most common in reporting suspicions of abuse, they are not the only ones who take action in protecting a child's well-being and safety. Among professionals, there are physicians, legal and law enforcement personnel.[8] Other sources who are courageous enough to stand up for children's safety were nonprofessionals such as friends, family, and neighbors.

Physical maltreatment is the easiest type of abuse to detect simply because there are physical attributes that are visible to the plain eye such as scars, cuts, burns and bruises that lead one to question the child's safety at home or wherever they spend most of their time. Warning signs of abuse and neglect are very noticeable in children. Things to look for are unexplained injuries, changes in behavior, regression, fear of going home, changes in eating and sleeping habits, changes in school performance and attendance, lack of personal care and hygiene, participating in risk taking behaviors, and displaying inappropriate sexual behaviors.[9] These are all warning signs that a child is being abused. Behavior changes are most common where children tend to lash out and act out because they

---

[8] https://www.childwelfare.gov/pubs/factsheets/canstats.cfm

[9] http://www.safehorizon.org/index/what-we-do-2/child-abuse--incest-55/10-signs-of-child-abuse--neglect-305.html

can't express their feelings in a reasonable manner. Other warning signs include improper dress for the weather, excessive bandages, excessively worn or torn clothing and shoes and excessive fear or flinching from particular movements.

Abuse can be prevented. It just takes people who are courageous enough to come forward and advocate for children's safety when there are suspicions of maltreatment.

There are many ways one can help reduce the number of children being abused. The best thing is to take action and report any suspicions that you may have that a child is being abused. If a child does come to you and tells you that he or she is being hit or bothered in an uncomfortable way, the best thing to do is listen to the child. Show the child that they have your concern and reassure them that you believe them and are available for support.[10]

If everyone had access to proper resources nationwide, the decline in known incidents would continue to decrease. More

---

[10] http://www.safehorizon.org/index/what-we-do-2/child-abuse--incest-55/10-signs-of-child-abuse--neglect-305.html

investigations would prevent people from wanting to risk their freedom and their child from being removed from their home. Hopefully, the increase in investigations would shed some light on some parents and help them realize that their child or children deserve better treatment and take some sort of action in becoming a better parent. There is a way to report child abuse suspicions in every state whether it is by contacting local authorities by phone or visiting a child safety website or by contacting their local department of health and human services.[11] It is critical to a child's development that they are nurtured. Anything can be classified as abuse. Excessive yelling and arguing around a child is not healthy. Releasing anger and frustration out on a child is going to lead to the child feeling ashamed, sad and guilty for reasons they don't know or understand. We can all do our part in advocating children's safety and wellness. All it takes is keeping a watchful eye and paying attention. The resources are available. Let's use them.

　　　-*Alisha Donald, Mother, Child Advocate*

---

[11]
https://www.childwelfare.gov/pubs/reslist/rl_dsp.cfm?rs_id=5&rate_chno=11-11172

Fatherhood, Trauma, and the Effect on Their Relationships

A man who is participating fully in all aspects of their children's lives emotionally, physically and financially, can be, by right, be considered a father. Could be biological, stepfathers, grandfathers/and or male caregivers, as long as they have strong, emotional connections with their children.

Fatherhood is defined by one's expectations, personal beliefs and value system. The style and choice of a father's caregiver behaviors are embedded deeply within his own experience of his father-child relationship. Father's care-giving style reflects selected imitation of and identification with how he was cared for by his father. Boys are learning how to be in a father role even with the absence of a father /father figure. Regardless of the circumstances, most boys think about how they will be as a father to their children. Each father's individual experience impacts the role and responsibility within the child rearing dyad.

The male is viewed as the protector of the family and often this role is shifted to the young males in the home who do not have the maturity and experience to handle this role.

The development of the father-child relationship is also impacted by cultures, societal influence, the man's own expectations, personal beliefs and value systems. Commitment refers to the strength of one's intention to participate and continue the relationships. When men become fathers under the influence of drugs, alcohol and prescription drugs, most likely a connection and a commitment has not been established and/or discussed with his partner. There is a likelihood of numerous partners. This circumstance does not alleviate fathers' responsibility to their children.

Research clearly indicate that fathers have strong influence on their child's overall emotional, social, and intellectual development. His presence and attention to his children have short and long term benefits. The absence of his care seems to affect his child's development. For example, children's academic achievement and IQ levels may be affected by the absence of a positive father-child relationship. Fathers influence social and sex-role development and serve as role models in their daily interactions with their children. (Park, 1981, Pruett 1987)

Many fathers feel poorly prepared for the task of parenting and childcare responsibilities. Many fathers reported considerable anxiety, confusion, and uneasiness over the many needs of their children. – Source: Spieler, 1982 and Nannarone 1983.

Origin of male trauma - The basic concept of trauma is based on childhood neglect and abuse statistics that includes physical, emotional/mental and sexual abuse.

What is trauma?

Trauma is defined as an event that overwhelms a person's ability to use normal coping mechanisms to adapt to everyday life situations and is disruptive to a person's frame of reference.

Trauma may occur in two ways: Direct experience or second hand (vicarious) experiences such as hearing accounts of violence. Substance Abuse disorders is defined as a pattern of use of alcohol/drugs (street/prescription drugs) which interfere with an individual's social, occupational, legal, financial, emotional, physical functioning.

There is limited research for men who report any type of trauma. My references to trauma are based on a research report by Dr. William C. Holmes of the University Of Pennsylvania School Of Medicine, about boys that have either been physically abused, emotionally neglected, and/or sexually abused.

Brief statistics – Based on the Fourth National Incidence Study of child abuse and neglect report to Congress prepared by the US Department of Health and Human Services Administration for Children and

Families (ACF) Office of Planning, Research, and Evaluation (OPRE), and the Children's Bureau – National Incidence of harm standard maltreatment in the Nis (2005 – 2006) indicated that in the following Perpetrator categories is the following:

Perpetrator category – biological parent 77.5
Out of home biological parent 3.3%
In-home step parent 3.2%
In-home non biological parents (foster, adoptive, etc.)
Other out of home non biological parent 0.1%
Parent's boyfriend or girlfriend 2.4%
Other family members 3.6%
Other unrelated adults 3.0%

Boys' responses to traumatic events vary depending on the circumstance, number of times, years of being neglected and abuse without protection from a trusted adult. When the perpetrator is a one of the parents, relative or a stranger, the impact of the trauma is more severe. When sexually abused boys are not treated, society must later deal with the resulting problems including crime, suicide, drug use and more sexual abuse said Dr. William C. Holmes of the University of Pennsylvania School Of Medicine.

Earlier studies found that of the one-third of juvenile delinquents, 40% are sexual offenders, and 76% of serial rapists' report they were sexually abused as youngsters. The suicide rate among sexually abused boys was 1.5% to 14 times higher, and reports of multiple substance abuse among sixth grade boys who were molested was 12 to 40 times greater.

Abuse and Neglect

(Source: Finkelhor et al, 1990)

In the adult retrospective study, victimization was reported as 27 percent of the women and 16 percent of the men. The median age for the occurrence of reported abuse was 9.9 years old for boys and 9.6 years old for girls. Victimization occurred before the age of eight for 22 percent of boys and for 23 percent for girls. Most of the abuse for both boys and girls was by offenders 10 or more years older than their victims. Girls were more likely than boys to disclose the abuse and 42% of the women and 33% of the men reported never having disclosing the experience to anyone. Men and boys don't generally report abuse – especially sexual abuse because it can be viewed as taboo- signs of weakness/ not being manly.

Factors Related to Men with Childhood Neglect & Abuse

Lowered Self-Worth – lack of confidence – promiscuous (using sex to feel confident)
Depression – sadness, reluctance to seek professional support due to stigmatization (undiagnosed mental illness/minor –major)
Post-traumatic stress disorder symptoms – acting out sexually and violently, very aggressive - acute stress that limits ability to participate fully in treatment and other activities
Childhood physical abuse may be a marker for other adult living conditions such as living in chaotic home environments. Other variables include age, sex, educational

attainment of parent or parents, alcohol or drug use in the home or neighborhood, presence of siblings or involvement of child protective services.

Dysfunctional Family Environments - Multiple lifetime sexual partners – resulting in having multiple children with multiple partners, sexually transmitted diseases.

Legal trouble –legal troubles begin, at what age, frequency.

Incarceration – did the trouble begin during early adolescence/juvenile delinquency?

Boys with childhood physical abuse histories was associated with depression and Post-traumatic stress disorder symptoms, incarceration, legal troubles, and a number of lifetime sexual partners.

Impact of Sexual Abuse and Neglect:

Long term effects of child abuse include fear, anxiety, depression, anger, hostility, inappropriate sexual behavior, poor self-esteem, tendency toward substance abuse and difficulty with close relationships. (Source: Brown & Finkelhor, 1986)

Sadly, a lack of nurture likewise affects brain development but in ways that may permanently increase a child's vulnerability to depression, stress, social isolation, and other negative outcomes.

Separation and Reunification - Father Instability

Homelessness - moving from place to place

Little or no income (low or no employment)

Rely on others for monetary support

Relapse

Frequent use of substances to cope with trauma

Harmful to self and others — violence may be a part of the active using phase

Unresolved feelings and emotions

Anger and resentment at self and mothers of children

Age of child trigger past childhood and adult trauma events

Limited opportunities to re-establish father-child connections

Child support issues

Mothers, extended family and friends influence on mother of children regarding reunification

Loss of contact with child's mom

Does not know mother of children

Lack of Knowledge - Father

Lack knowledge on the true effect of parental substance use – too numb to feel due to trauma

Lack knowledge on health status – sexually transmitted diseases, e.g. HIV, AIDS

Self-Care Skills

Poor or low esteem – uncaring about appearance

Personal hygiene

Lack access to health care or ignore medical needs for long periods of time – preventable sickness/dental

Lack knowledge on healthy nutrition

Effective Discipline Practices
May have adopted the same coercive strategies when they were abused in an attempt to control their child's behavior. Power Over is the method for developing relationships

Use of guilt to control behavior

Inability to calm and soothe self and children (agitated state)

Constantly in a state of being overwhelmed by own needs and societal expectations instead of reality

Children's Developmental Tasks
Little or no knowledge on what to expect from child

Lack knowledge on addressing child's emotional needs

Role reversal – child is feeling responsible for how father is feeling instead of father paying attention to child's emotional state.

Needs of Children
Lack of physical emotional and financial support and access to child

Lack of involvement in child's activities – school based sports, extra curricula and/or community work

Difficulty paying attention to children's needs – enmeshed needs – difficulty in separating own needs and children's needs – important for staff to understand when offering support for child that the parent may reject support services because he may feel that they don't need it which leads to a father having difficulty recognizing the needs of their child. Not intentional ⁻ difficulty addressing own needs

Lack empathy

Problem Solving Skills

Difficulty addressing problems

Power over instead of power – may use power as the standard for developing relationships instead of/win/win

Underdeveloped sense of mastery over problem-solving skills

Conflict Resolution Skills

Poor communication skills and styles

Tend to confront with anger and frustration

Mimic child's behavioral affect — hurting the child's feelings

Social & Emotional Development

Lack of or under-developed self-regulation functions (father)

Isolation — does not develop a support system for fear that others will learn about issues at home — reluctant to join or establish close relationships

May avoid parenting children who are the same age as the father's traumatic experience or hyper-vigilant/overprotective for fear of injury to child

Low paternal attachment — repeated exposure to parents fluctuating emotional state- father and child not sure how to respond to each other

Establishing, Implementing & Maintaining Routines

Difficulty developing a realistic schedule with primary care takers

Unaware of no or low cost age appropriate activities for children
Difficulty maintaining a commitment to continuing consistent routines with child

Emotional Disconnections between Parent & Child Caused by:
Undeveloped Relationships
Fear of rejection/commitment
Afraid to build relationships
Lack experience in being in a nurturing parent-child relationship
Lack empathy for children feelings and circumstances
Isolation
Depression

Emotional Effects of Use & Withdrawal from Substances
Shame and guilt
Physical pain (headaches)
Cravings

Difficulty Maintaining Trust
Don't' trust or use own judgment – difficulty trusting others – family

members – rely on others for decision making – follower - Lack trust in self
Inconsistent
Not reliable

Possible Impacts of Substance Use Disorders on Children's Behaviors

Impulsive Behavior – stealing, lying

Lack of Internalized Image of right and wrong – wasn't given sufficient guidance, possible mental health issues hindering true understanding

Frequently Seen as "Acting Out" – labeled the "the Bad boy/kid"- frequently misunderstood by others around him – always hear someone calling out his name in different settings - school & home

Unhealthy, Maladaptive Roles in Family- passive aggressive

Unhealthy coping strategies – fighting, physical, throwing, difficult to calm down

Numbing – Don't Feel – use disassociation as a coping mechanism

Poor Self-Regulation Skills – may wet the bed at night – easily over stimulated

Difficulty to Calm and Self-Soothe – lack skills or do not have the internal ability to calm down on own and self-soothe without support –

Shame and Guilt – experience a strong and complex level of shame and guilt over parents behaviors

Poor or undeveloped socialization skills – more frequently with boys

Dysfunctional relationships – lack positive, appropriate role models

Un-Grieved losses

Boys – Speech, Behavior, Conduct Disorders

children

Daniels Story

I am going to introduce you to Daniel. Some elements of this story are not included on purpose. The goal of this activity is to provide you a snapshot of a typical man/father recovering from trauma and substance abuse.

Family of Origin

Daniel is a 28 year old father of 5 children ranging in age 12 to 3 years old, with 5 different women. He has a high school diploma. He lives with his girlfriend Stacey, who is 25 years old, and their 3 year old son named Jacob. Daniel's occupation before entering into a 6 month residential substance abuse treatment facility for men was a warehouse worker. From the age of three, he was sexually and physically abused by his stepfather until he was seven years old. His mom emotionally and physically abused him as well because of his aggressive behaviors toward other children. His mom was a closet alcoholic and stay at home mother. His stepfather was a highly respected, successful barbershop owner in their community. Daniel started experimenting with alcohol and cigarettes at age 9 as a means to cope with his home environment.

The school was concerned about his academic, behavior, safety and overall well-being and filed a case with the Child Protection Service agency. The case was substantiated and he was removed from his home when he was 12. He lived in foster care until he was 19 with no contact with his mother. He got a job working at a local warehouse. Daniel met Stacey at work. She was a secretary at the same warehouse. This was Daniel and Stacey's first time being in a long term, committed relationship. Daniel wanted to raise his children differently from his own up-bringing but his recovery program did not offer any parenting education and support information.

What losses did Daniel experience as a result of childhood history?

Some losses – include protection, confidence/trust/self-esteem/lack of self-control/lacked positive parenting experiences, loss of innocence, loss of contact with other children, positive school involvement experience, nurturing loving relationship with mom, participation in school activities.

Healthy Grieving Processes

Healthy grieving has five components that can overlap and have back and forth movement between them. I added Time because it is critical to allow a sufficient amount of time for consumers to recover and understand what is happening to them.

__Denial__ – refusal to believe the loss either in outright statement e.g. I don't believe it) or in behavior; continuing do routines based on the person being in their life even though they left them.

__Anger__ – at the person lost, or causing the loss (themselves) sometimes this is a feeling of betrayal or of being let down; sometimes it is a feeling of fury of being left.

__Bargaining__ – trying to find a way to undo the loss. This can sometimes be part of an internal dialogue by talking to yourself or asking your higher power to undo the loss. It can take the form of actively trying to negotiate someone or something's return, and often has flavor of trying to put things the way they used to be.

__Depression__ – A loss of interest, appetite, energy; a sense of being overwhelmed by the loss or losses and by the need to cope in the face of the loss. At this point, some people worry about their sanity and wonder if life will ever be better.

Acceptance/Adjustment – the final stage, where reality of the loss is understood and adaptation – adjustment begins to occur. The reality is accepted that life can/will be different, but it also will/can be good.

Time- added because a father with a history of trauma needs more time to adjust to the events and accept all of the many changes occurring at rapid speed.

Grief- part of early sobriety because people lose the powerful relationships that they had with the alcohol or drug abuse and with the lifestyle, in addition to beginning to understand the losses resulting from substance use. This process leads to healing.

Interventions- relearned emotional /self-regulation skills, enter a treatment program that can address trauma and substance abuse, parenting. Programs can incorporate father friendly treatment protocols. By beginning with the development of building healthy and strong relationships.

Principles of Relational Development

Authenticity is the freedom and ability to live within a relationship at a high level of exposure and vulnerability
Mutuality means that energy and interest flow back and forth between two people and is characterized by a dynamic, interactive sensitivity and responsiveness
Empathy is the process by which disclosure and sharing on oneself leads to a heightened sense of self and understanding others.

Humans are hardwired to form relationships. Our biological systems predispose human beings to form and sustain enduring, nurturing relationships. Based on studies of both animals and humans, neuroscientists have come to understand that a complex systems of hormones and other chemical messengers in the brain guides how we react to what's happening to and around us.

Making or creating direct connection between **_what we say or feel and what we do was seen as_** important in understanding how healthy relationships are fostered.

Most men confessed that admitting that they had a problem and it was difficult for them to ask for help because from a societal standpoint there is an inordinate amount of pressure to deny the presence of problems or deficits.

Significant changes need to be made in how programs/staff receive and welcome men and boys into services offered.

Work with families of boys to assist them in thinking about how they teach them social skills so that their messages facilitate their healthy development without conflicting expectations.

Men Relational Development
Reinforce nurturing behavior in human males –

Studies indicate that similar hormonal feedback loops reinforce nurturing behavior in human males. When a man becomes involved in a sustained committed intimate relationship, his testosterone level – thus his biological drive toward aggression and promiscuity – actually goes down significantly.

Lack of information and education about what are the ingredients of a healthy relationship- involving sexual intimacy and how to develop a healthy relationship that includes sexual intimacy impacted the perpetration of intimate partner violence. The image of masculinity and conforming to stereotypical gender roles were identified as contributing factors to the development of poor relationship skills. It is clear that one's social context affects one's understanding of, and attention to, what constitutes a healthy relationship. There are instances where adults could address behaviors that were negative but ignored them because "boys will be boys."

For thousands of years we have recognized the importance of nurture in forming a child's character, but neuroscience is now beginning to show that the positive effects of nurture goes much deeper, actually shaping a child's brain in way that will provide lifelong health benefits. For better or worse, the presence or absence of early nurture actually affects a child's brain circuitry. The results become hardwired in a way that can profoundly affect lifelong behavior. While new research is looking for ways to enrich older children' nurturing environment to compensate for early deficits, it is clear that early investment in supportive nurturing pays lifelong dividends.

Nurture the Child
Structure & Consistency
An opportunity to adjust to recovering parent

Time to re-establish trust in their parents or caregiver

Empathic & Nurturing Responses
Responses are age appropriate and kind

Modeling for future behaviors

Personal Growth

Developmental appropriate information about addiction and recovery

To be taught how to identify and allow to express feelings about their experience in a safe place

Coping Skills – taught by parents, caregivers and trusted adults

Consistent routines support the development of internal emotional regulation

Opportunities to Enhance Self-Esteem- set limits that are loving age appropriate discipline from caregivers

Allow Mistakes – the freedom to make mistakes without condemnation or physical or emotional punishment

Praise/Acknowledgement – focus on positive behaviors – strength-based approaches – what can you do

Creativity & Fun

Recreational activities outside of the home

Increased positive interactions and communication between parents, children, siblings and peers –praise at every opportunity. These interactions build social coping skills.

Supervision (different ages requires different levels)

Strong commitment and follow-through from both parents to maintain on-going contact and communication.

Intervention Strategies

Fathers need interventions that are relational and family centered. Professionals can support fathers with substance and trauma issues by providing:

Hope

A safe and nurturing environment to begin the healing process recovery issues for survivors includes getting control of event in the victim's/survivors mind, working out an understanding of the event and, as needed a redefinition of values, re-establishing a new equilibrium/life, re-establishing trust, re-establishing a future and re-establishing meaning of the event – men need to have an opportunity to experience this process.

Support in Developing a Positive Self-Image as a Parent
Step-by-Step Instructions
An Opportunity to Grieve

Fathers Need- Coordinated support to work effectively with Child Protective Services, Child Support Agency, Legal system and other ancillary supports

Interagency collaboration, coordinated and integrated case management
Interpretation of service plan when families are involved with multi-agencies

Father Focused Age Appropriate Activities – Positive social orientation – engage in enjoyable events that are no cost or low cost – take into consideration that men place high value on being able to pay for activities

Parenting Education and Support Programs

Group-based setting can support men in acknowledging their need for support

Screen for history of child and/or adulthood trauma and substance use disorder

All fathers groups should include a male facilitator

There are many ways for all of us to help, we just have to be willing to do so.

- *Tanji Donald, Educator, Lecturer*

CHAPTER 7

STRESS AND SOCIETY

.

"Living is the constant process of deciding what you are going to do."
-Jose Ortega y Gasset

The Effects of Stress and Psychological Disorder

When it comes to psychological disorders, there are several methods used to reach a consensus and properly diagnose a patient. Medical professionals must record a history of the patient's life and a family history to determine whether a condition is genetic. Each individual must then be analyzed and assessed, as each case is conceptualized so a proper diagnosis can be made. From that diagnosis, treatment will be recommended, and the patient should be on their way to living a healthier life with their disorder or illness.

As different cases are reviewed, one will find that each individual is diagnosed according to the relativity of very specific symptoms. For each diagnosis of major depression and anxiety disorders, stressors usually play a large role in the onset of the disorder.

Major depression disorder is a chronic disorder that is characterized by having a low mood and is usually in conjunction with low self-esteem. People who suffer from major depression typically have down periods where they want to be alone, sometimes displaying a shy and introverted demeanor because their level of self-esteem is low.

One of the main causes for major depressive disorder is everyday life stressors. The happiest people can experience a traumatic or even a seemingly normal experience and it may onset a downward spiral of mood and lack of self-esteem. Everyday stressors are classified as things that normally occur in everyday life like bills, children, work, and school. If these stressors are compounded with the abuse of drugs and alcohol, means by which some people try to cope, the recipe for disaster becomes more enhanced and problematic. Some of these things may cause too heavy of a burden on a person at any given time.

Anxiety disorders are also heightened when stressors come into play. Anxiety is a feeling of increased nervousness and heightened emotions. When we think of things that make us anxious, we think of speaking in front of large groups, meeting people for the first time, going for a job interview and other things of a social nature. People who are diagnosed with anxiety disorders typically are diagnosed that way because of how they were evaluated and what the psychologist scored them as.

These are just two examples of stress related disorders, and in both cases, the level of stress greatly affects how a person reacts to any situation. A person who is diagnosed with stress related disorder typically has some sort of reaction where whatever they try to do to overcome their symptoms fails because the disorder has reached the point of affecting how they function on a daily basis. Once this happens, some form of medical attention is needed. A person in this state must be helped, not pushed aside or forgotten about.

Here is an example of how an unforeseen circumstance can compromise the mental wherewithal of a seemingly normal person. A woman becomes widowed and has to take on a second job in order to provide for her two children. There is high demand of her work schedule and she is always scrambling to make ends meet. Over time, she begins to feel more and more flustered by the demands imposed on her and the death of her spouse, and she begins to have migraines. One day she begins to feel sad about her situation and starts to cry excessively. Her children don't know how to react because their mom always seemed so headstrong. Eventually, the mother seeks help because she does not want her children to see her in such an unusual state.

She confesses to her physician that there have been several times over the past few months that she did not even want to get out of her bed because it seemed as though her days never ended. She was diagnosed with a stress related disorder because the stressors of everyday life caused her to retreat. She was unable to function without periodic bouts of crying and immobility.

For the majority of psychological disorders, there is more often than not, underlying stress factors that play a part in elevating the symptoms and causing the onset of a more major disorder.

Some of these stressors, which can be clear and direct, while others are more subtle, can lead a person to be socially paralyzed. Some researchers even assert that constant stress can disrupt our physical well-being, and makes us more susceptible to colds and other ailments.

Here, I find it relevant to present a list of stressors that are the main causes of psychological disorders.

Work-related problems
Because work is central in most people's lives, the effects of unemployment or of a chronically stressful work environment can be especially severe.

Noise

Children who live or go to school in noisy, urban areas have higher blood pressure and higher levels of stress hormones, are more distractible, and have more learning and attention difficulties than do children in quieter environments (Cohen et al., 1980; Evans, Bullinger, & Hygge, 1998). In adults, constant loud noise contributes to cardiovascular problems, irritability, fatigue, and aggressiveness (Staples, 1996).

Bereavement and Loss

In the two years following bereavement, widowed people, especially men, are more susceptible to illness and physical ailments, and their mortality rate is higher than would otherwise be expected (Stroebe, Stroebe, & Schut, 2001).

Poverty, Powerlessness, and Low Status

People at the lower rungs of the socioeconomic ladder have worse health and higher mortality rates for almost every disease and medical condition than do those at the top (Adler & Snibbe, 2013). In America, one obvious reason is that poor people cannot afford medical care. They are also more likely to eat high-calorie, fast-food diets that increase the chances of obesity and diabetes. Another reason for the poorer health of low-income people is that they often live with continuous environmental stressors- higher crime rates, discrimination, fewer community services, run-down housing, and greater exposure to hazards such as chemical contamination-and the constant emotional stressors of fear, anxiety, and anger (Gallo & Matthews, 2003) These conditions disproportionately affect urban black people and may help account for a higher rate of hypertension, which can then lead to kidney disease, strokes, and heart attacks (Clark et al., 1999).

In considering these things, we as people have to understand that individual complications in life are highly likely to become complications for society as a whole. We cannot believe that personal problems do not lead to social problems, and visa-versa. Our world is made up of people, *real people*, and anytime we disregard the fact that each person faces various circumstances that alter the way their minds can process solutions or a means to cope, we as a society cannot look forward to the root word of disorder. Our minds matter.

-*Alisha Donald, Researcher, Human Servant*

CHAPTER 8

TRUE FREEDOM AND EQUALITY

*"Every problem provides an opportunity
for you to do your best."*
-Duke Ellington

POWER: WHAT IT MEANS TO PEOPLE

Power, by its mean definition, has many aspects that equal a whole, all-encompassing meaning. In summation, power in its truest form means: the capacity to influence the behavior of others, the emotions of others, or any course of events that may directly or indirectly affect others.

I have formulated a list of the well-known attributes of power. It is my sincere plea to all who read this that you think on these things and try to understand why an excessive amount of power or a significant lack thereof, transforms the world in which we live into an unsure place.

Attributes of Power

- The ability to do something unchecked
- Political authority
- National and International influence
- Military strength (show of force)
- Possession of land and resources
- Economic and financial prosperity; the commercial strength to compete locally and globally
- The means to advance scientifically and technologically
- Medical and healthcare resources
- The capability to respond effectively to crises and natural disaster
- The means to provide an education that is both practical and purposeful

The aforementioned attributes of power are what constitutes a nation. To abuse or disregard any of these aspects of power disrupts a nation's infrastructure and leads to an imbalance in society as a whole. There is a tremendous responsibility that comes with power, and any person or persons who are lax in this responsibility should be stripped of their power, plain and simple.

A society cannot possess land and natural resources and disregard the environment or the people who inhabit it. We cannot have the means to advance scientifically and technologically, and utilize this capability only to manufacture weaponry and genetically alter foodstuffs, while the average child from the inner city drinks water from a faucet that does not come close to meeting the EPA standard. This is illogical.

This is our problem. The marginalized people of this country have no power. Our power has either been wrested away from us, or, we never had it in the first place. The dilemma that stems from this gross encroachment upon the dignity of the powerless, is that it churns us into an expendable blob; numbers, statistics and probabilities that can be categorized and placed in an index that those with power deem fit.

The intrepid force of the "spirit killers", those who place purse before person, have always laid out an open invitation to hell to those of us who make no effort to learn, know, strive, and change. They have a place for the rebellious; those who tell the ones with the power to share the world, the resources, the rights of humankind.

The historian, Bernard Lewis, pointed it out as clear as I have ever heard it. He states:

"That to be strong, one must be prosperous, and to be prosperous, one must be free."

Being physically free is the least of our freedoms. I know brothers and sisters who are incarcerated physically throughout the world, and they will be the first to tell anyone that freedom is priceless, but knowledge is twice that. When we as people realize that there are systems in place that can take away or limit our physical freedom, then we must believe in our own capabilities to stand far away from these traps, until we build up the power to change these systems.

My father told me, before his untimely death in 1987, that "the strongest people are not the ones with the most scars, but the ones who know they are gonna' get hit, so they hit first." A die-hard boxing fan was he. Back then, I could not fully understand what he was trying to tell me, because I thought that if you "took a licking and kept on ticking," you had proven yourself, at least in the sense of a physical fight.

In the here and now, I think I have an idea as to what my pops, the broad-shouldered son of a sharecropper from the backwoods of Tennessee, was trying to tell me, and if he shifts in his grave after I write this, I pray that it is a nod of approval.

The strongest people amongst us are those who begin the round of life with the odds overwhelmingly stacked against them, and upon *knowing* this, they properly arm themselves and go on the offensive, building strength and power in the process.

They arm themselves with a proper education. They strengthen their bodies and minds with the proper nutrition necessary to live. They instill the qualities and virtues of being efficient, compassionate, and humble into their families and loved ones. They exercise their right to be firm against foolishness and make manifest their intention to better themselves and their community.

They respect power, so they do not use it to punish, rather they use it to bust the bully's nose and show the other kids in the schoolyard that, yes and it can be done. *Yes we can stand up against the powers that be.*

<u>*Taking a Chance on Change*</u>

In honor of the esteemed leaders who have made sacrifices beyond measure, and in the spirit of service, I find it relevant here to attempt to reclaim the fire that comes with struggle. With the triumphs comes the setbacks; with the good comes the rush of all things bad.

It strikes me odd that Dr. Martin Luther King Jr., one of the most endearing, and passionate leaders of the 20th century somehow became this almost mythical, arch mage of peace, rather than being celebrated as a true freedom fighter, a *man* who sought to change the world with thoughts, words and actions, and not just rhetoric and hope.

My voice and my words may resonate with some, maybe all people who feel that life has dealt them some serious blows in regards to seeking equality. However, I cannot, and will not attempt to make this journey myself. Instead, it is my desire to activate the voices of the people whom the sacrifices of Dr. King have and will continue to help the most.

Dr. King took a chance on change, and like him, we all owe it to ourselves to take up the reins and push our steeds of humanity to the limit, without compromising our sense of compassion for other people's lives.

My ten year old daughter recently wrote a piece about Dr. King for a fifth grade assignment. I noted that she wrote what she believed to be an accurate depiction of Dr. King's life. I was stunned to discover that she did what a lot of us adults do not do: She regarded him as a human being. Not a martyr, but a man. Not a hero, but a father. Not a revolutionary, but a reverend.

These aspects of Dr. King's life are often overshadowed by his legacy and his death. As true as I can put it, one cannot curtail Dr. King's accomplishments, no way, no how. But we must keep in perspective *why* he did what he did, rather than focusing on the outcome. Focusing on the result not only leaves a lot to be desired, for we still live in a world where minorities are discriminated against, but it subtracts from the fact that Dr. King fought for his life and the lives of others, until he died for it.

With certainty, I tried in earnest not to revise my daughter's work, but as punctuation and spelling would have it, I conjured up the editor in me and took it to task.

A Man Who Changed Things
By Cherish CowanRaye

Martin Luther King Jr. was a man who changed things. He led peaceful marches for civil and human rights. He gave speeches and helped more people become voters.

Even though sometimes he was placed in jail, he never gave up, and remained peaceful. During one march where Dr. King and others were sprayed with water hoses and attacked by police dogs, they still prayed for their enemies, hoping that non-violence would win to make people equal.

During those times, white people thought they were better than black people because of their skin color and did not want to share anything with them. I could not imagine how Dr. King and other black people felt back then, but I know it would have hurt my feelings.

Like Dr. King, I feel that we are all humans and should be treated the same. I am grateful that Dr. King dedicated his life to opening people's eyes to things like racism. It inspires me to treat people fairly, no matter what race they are, where they come from, or what they look like.

I had a dream that cookies and cake fell from the sky, and maybe some licorice, and every person on the planet walked hand in hand to have a party and talk about human rights.

AFTERWORD

I must say that all things have *meaning*, but not all things have value. The value of some particular thing must find its origin in the purpose it serves and what benefit we derive from it. For example, the relationship between an infection and our immune system *means* that we may become sick. Where is the value in that for us?

I argue from the perspective of applying the principle of value, or the *ideal* of value, to our society. In other words, if we can envision a concept of society that is built on true equality, and one that we can actually turn into a reality, that concept has tremendous value; not only to an individual, but to ALL people, because the possibility or the hope of a better society is valuable.

Value is in what we produce. All of our ideas are productions, blueprints for constructs that can not only be tangible things, but useful things. Therefore, the worth of something can be found in the how and why it was produced in the first place and its usefulness.

When funds that support social services are reallocated, when the costs of living continue to rise, and when new zoning laws confirm the expansion of commercial properties rather than residential, we as people must understand that these incidences are the ideas of other people who embody certain systems and institutions. They believe in their ideas; they believe in their utility. Their bold impositions assert that the expense of many should benefit the few; they lie for it, steal for it, even kill for it, this ideal of theirs, their values.

We as people have to disagree with the state of our society, based on the things that have been clearly established and demonstrated. We must argue that necessity is the precursor to value, and because value is not a commodity, no one can buy or sell justice. No system or set of systems should have the power or authority to bang our rights into nothingness.

Our needs as people must be met. One of these needs is equality, plain and simple. Almost every other need can be branched to true equality. No one system can give a person or group of people a sense of equality, we have to feel it and exercise it. Unfortunately, a system can withhold or take away this sense of equality by enforcing the concepts of class, race, socioeconomic status, gender, and any other name tag they can apply to place people in a specific category. Once categorized, we as people become "easier to deal with"; guppies in an ocean full of bloodthirsty, predatory Mako sharks.

Our country has a history of inequality that continues to stratify our lives into unreliable, erratic layers of existence. There are inner-city children, right now, who have no park to play in, while "dog parks" are being landscaped everyday where an animal can urinate, frolic, and chase their tails.

Dear Reader, we owe it to ourselves to nurture our dignity; we owe it to our children to, "Learn. Know. Strive. Change."

ABOUT THE AUTHOR

Leonard Swafford-Donald, Author and President of Master Builder Publications, is a lecturer, and a former prisoner.

Mr. Swafford-Donald has been hailed by one social commentator as, "a new voice that speaks provocatively concerning issues of race and social structures."

His firsthand knowledge of classism and racial disparities while growing up in the inner-city of Boston, Massachusetts, has spurned him to action and is reflected in his works.

"I was born in the 70's, raised in the 80's, lost in the 90's, and incarcerated for the first twelve and a half years of the new millennium; my life itself is a stark testament to ignorance, cycles of oppression, losses and triumphs, order and chaos."

Mr. Swafford-Donald has committed his time and energy to educating himself and others, while at the same time establishing Master Builder Publications as a literary force to be reckoned with.

"I write to expose social ills, not to expose individuals. It is not my desire to injure the force that controls the machine. My desire is to dismantle the machine, and take away the power of that force."

The Broken Clock: An Examination of People and Society is his third book.

For more info, please visit *www.masterbuilderpublications.com*

Leonard Swafford-Donald

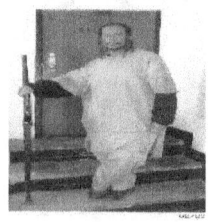

J. JABIR POPE

WILLIAM "KASIM" LANE

JEFFREY ANTHONY

ZACHARIAH IBRAHIM BUSH

DEBORAH RAYE

LEONARD SWAFFORD-DONALD

ALEX "FLACO" GARCIA

ALISHA DONALD

ALEX JEANTY

CHERISH COWAN RAYE

STEPHEN P. ENGLEY

TANJI DONALD

MARY ELLEN FLANNERY

NAEEM MILES

MASTER BUILDERS EMPOWERMENT GROUP

THE WISE BILL HIMELHOCH